PICTURE BOOK
OF
BRITAIN
IN COLOUR

PICTURE BOOK
OF
BRITAIN
IN COLOUR

TREASURE PRESS

Editor's note: the old county names have been occasionally retained in order to allow the reader to locate the places mentioned with greater accuracy.

Half-title page: this stretch of coast in County Antrim, Northern Ireland, affords a spectacular view of the White Rocks and, beyond, of Dunluce Castle.

Title page: the spire of Holy Trinity Church, Stratford on Avon, rising above the trees and river, a scene which shows how this most celebrated of towns has retained its essentially rural atmosphere.

Opposite: five of Henry VIII's wives lived in Hampton Court, the palace which Cardinal Wolsey began and which remained a royal residence until the time of George III. Since then it has been a much-visited museum.

N 16934

First published in Great Britain in 1971 by
The Hamlyn Publishing Group Limited

This edition published in 1989 by
Treasure Press
Michelin House
81 Fulham Road
London SW3 6RB

ISBN 1 85051 428 3

Produced by Mandarin Offset
Printed and bound in Hong Kong

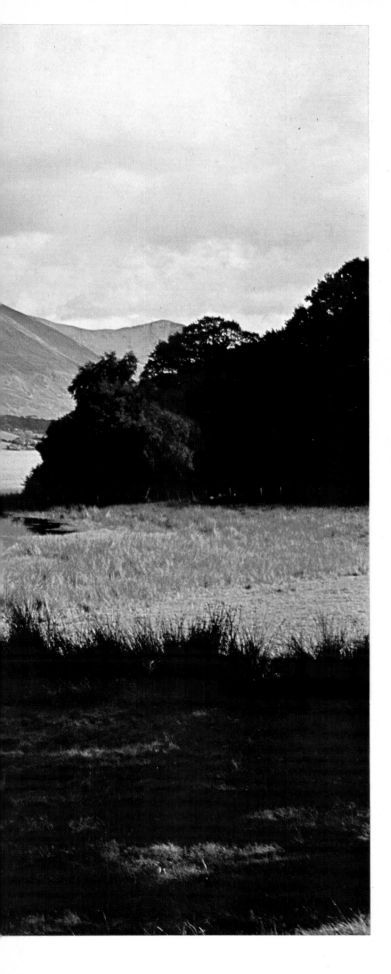

Contents

Loweswater in the Lake District, lesser known perhaps than many places in that region but here proving that it is no less worthy of attention, wearing its summer colours like a peacock.

Seashore

Rude, cruel, wine-dark, tempest-tossed . . . the poets' epithets for the sea have crashed or danced about our ears for centuries, and for those bred on these shores it must rank among the most favoured founts of inspiration. Not surprisingly. There must be few land masses in the world that have a coastline whose beauty and variety can equal that of Britain's, and even fewer for whom the coastline is so eminently accessible. We fortunates who inhabit these islands may easily forget that across the face of the great continents there are millions of people for whom the sight and sound and smell of the sea are untasted joys, millions more for whom the one experience of it has been a scruffy over-populated beach or an oil-scarred port. Yet here there is nowhere that is not within less than a day's drive of the great salt water. And the choice is infinite — beaches, bays, rocks, cliffs, coves, harbours, shingle, sand; gulches echoing with the suck and pull of the tides; pebbled beaches bleached smooth by salt and sun, where the high-water mark leaves slivers of seaweed draped across the stones; the great jagged seascapes of Cornwall where the western seas gnaw at the rock-face; those crumbling and sometimes cheese-yellow southern cliffs of chalk with their overgrown grassy tops; the wide curved sweep of Pembrokeshire bays that end in a tapering headland, and in whose waters may still be seen the rare pleasure of a family of seals; the crude saw-tooth'd outline of the Western Scottish coast with its wild sea-lochs and its haphazard collection of oddly-named islands; the North Sea beaches, long and empty, packed by dunes and tufted grass, whipped clean by the grey fury of the wind; the flat silver-streaked estuaries of the south-east where the sea birds flight in at dusk over the thin margin of land and pierce the darkness with their demonic cries; the fishing-boat-bobbing quays and harbours of the holiday havens, the beaches where once ignorant armies clashed by night and where now the summer bodies fight daily for a level stretch of sand.

Ignorant armies or not, once upon a time all visitors to Britain had to come by sea — Caesar waded through the shallows off the Kent coast, William marched stoutly up that Sussex beach, the Norsemen slid their great-prowed vessels across the sands at varying points north and east. Nowadays, more often

than not, the visitor is winged in across the skies and may see no more of the coast than a far-off creaminess at the land's edge or a necklace of lights briefly twinkling in some holiday resort. This chapter comes first in this book to redress the balance. Something of tradition, some demand for historical perspective, requires that the importance and the splendours of these seashores be acknowledged first of all.

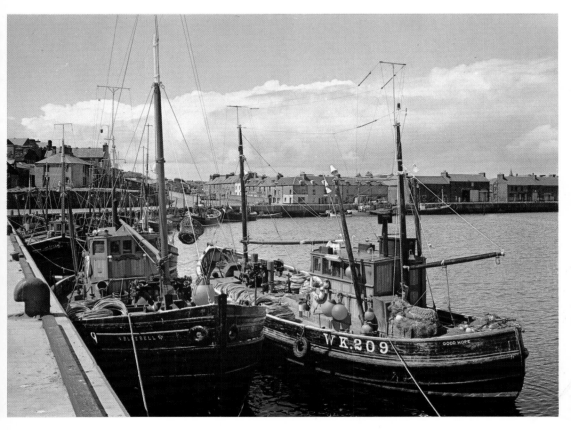

Far left: the coast of Essex with its creeks and inlets and long-winding estuaries still has an air of surreptitious invasion. The cockle boats unloading their catch onto the mudflats at Leigh-on-Sea are plying honourable trade, but these mazy waters that stretch so far inland have seen in their time the stealth of less legal invaders, those who have come by night and disturbed none but the teeming wildlife of this area.
Left: the fishing boats in the harbour at Wick, Caithness, are sturdy craft, built to ride out the inhospitality of the North Sea in search of herring, for which this town is a centre. A royal burgh, it also boasts a ruined castle to the south, one of many in this embattled corner of the land.
Previous page: fine unmolested sands near Durness, Sutherland, on the most northerly coastline of Britain — virtually unmolested, in fact, since the Norsemen arrived here in 1034, stayed for two centuries, and left without evidence of their occupation.

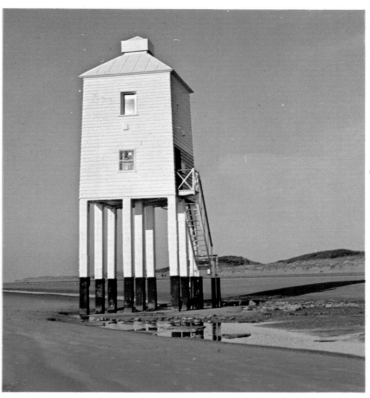

Had lighthouses existed in 1588 the Spanish Armada would no doubt have been saved a few galleons as they fled round the coast of Britain. Not even the extremities of the land were lit then. *Far left:* the northernmost point of the mainland is not John O'Groats but Dunnet Head, whose lighthouse rakes the Pentland Firth separating it from Hoy and the Orkney Islands, a stretch of water notorious for its treachery. Some 900 miles to the south and west is the Longships Lighthouse off Land's End (*centre*), which some still think of as the last stepping-stone before the Great Unknown.

Left: Burnham-on-Sea, Somerset, has two lighthouses, one conventional, the other this quaint and unforbidding watchtower on the sands.

Below: the stretch of coast round Portland Bill, Dorset, is well-known for the Pulpit Rock, the Chesil Bank, and not least for the handsome lighthouse on the Portland Bill promontory.

Left: the coastline at opposite ends of England. Embleton Bay with its broad sweep of sand and fringe of coarse grass is typical of the Northumberland seashore, perhaps the most romantic part of the country for those whose taste inclines to knights and castles and medieval warrings.

Dunstanburgh Castle, in the distance, is one of many such that stand crumbling in this northernmost English county; built in the 14th century and decaying since the 16th, it still affords a magnificent spectacle, and on days of bleak weather when the North Sea wind touches you like cold steel it is difficult not to feel the presence of ghosts from those bloody Border wars.

Above: Brixham Harbour in Devon, on the other hand, with its brightly painted trawlers could not present a cosier or more welcoming picture. William of Orange was no doubt glad of this when he landed here in 1688 to claim the Stuart throne, and a statue on the quay commemorates this fact. Sir Francis Drake, too, dropped anchor here with a captured Spanish galleon from the Armada, but less well-known perhaps is that it was within sight of this port that Napoleon embarked in *HMS Northumberland*, outward bound for his last exile on St Helena. Today Brixham remains resolutely sea-minded — the trawlers share the harbour with the pleasurecraft of holidaymakers, and the cries of the gulls still manage to outweigh the invading roar of traffic.

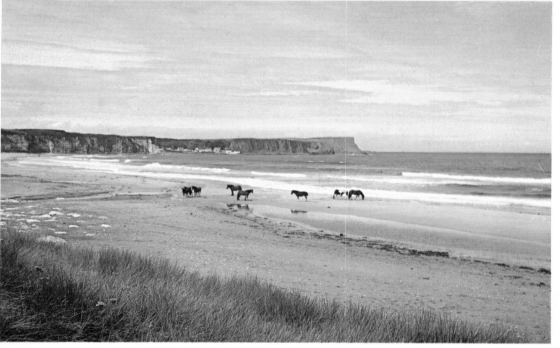

St Ives, Cornwall (*above*) has appealed to a diversity of characters all through its history, from the lady saint from Ireland who gave her name to the town, to Perkin Warbeck who landed here to begin his pursuit of Henry VII's throne. A little further west down the north Cornish coast the sea-borne traveller may meet with a more rough-hewn spectacle — the Botallack tin mine (*right*), near St Just-in-Penwith. Abandoned now to the Atlantic's battering, it is no more than a relic of Cornwall's busiest industrial period. Its appearance is deceptive, however, for the shaft descends over a thousand feet under the rock and far out under the sea.

Left: White Park Bay in County Antrim, Northern Ireland, and what could be more natural just around the headland from such a crazy phenomenon as the Giant's Causeway than that horses, not people, should inhabit the beach?

The music-hall tradition is not dead in Britain. In the steep and cobbled streets of Clovelly, Devon (*right*), you can apparently still see the rolling gait of a fisherman on his way back down to the sea. And Blackpool (*above*), famous, lovely Blackpool, 'queen of the resorts', has always featured, with affection, in the songs and jokes of the music-hall. This view, taken from the top of the celebrated Tower on a stormy evening, owes nothing to the equally celebrated illuminations which attract so many visitors to the town. But it shows another striking feature – the seafront – which extends for seven miles, crammed with every possible attraction that a holidaymaker could want. Even the more sedate members of the political conferences held here must find it hard not to be a little diverted by its raffish charms. Let it not be thought, either, that Clovelly, or the fisherman, if fisherman he be, are mocked. This village, tucked into the wide sweep of Bideford Bay, and one of the most beautiful in Devon, is known for the precipitousness of its streets, the descent of which require a rare balance.

18

A huddle of houses, a few slight boats, and the enclave of a harbour, walled against the sea. The coast of Britain has many such communities, defiant and self-protective in the winter, swollen with visitors in the summer. For all the upheaval that the latter causes the character of these places remains unaltered. St Abbs, Berwickshire (*far left, top*), in the Border country of Scotland, preserves a distilled calm beneath the 300 ft cliffs that well up behind it. It has long known how to take care of itself — those same cliffs are riddled with smugglers' caves. In Cornwall, too, from which the other two pictures come, there is a streak of canny resilience, part perhaps of the Celtic inheritance. Mousehole (*far left, bottom*) is well-named as it lies hidden behind an almost circular harbour wall, and Port Isaac (*left*), on the north coast of that county, looks virtually impregnable with its narrow sea-entrance and its guardian hills. To add to this impression of fortification, nearby are the remains of Castle Dameliock, the 'Castle Terrible' of the *Morte d'Arthur*.

London

Familiar friends in high places, enjoying a cleaner London air these days since the problems of pollution began to be tackled and America's idea of England's capital, as expressed in those fog-bound songs and smog-ridden movies, was banished. Trafalgar Square's Nelson (*below*), Piccadilly's Eros (*right*), the Old Bailey's Statue of Justice (*far right*), symbolic all three of some kind of conquest, now gleam with a new lustre on sunny days.
Previous page: it isn't just brilliant weather that commands the view. From one of London's newest pinnacles, the top of the GPO Tower, the vast expanse of the city lies carpeted beneath.

In practice, of course, all roads, rail-tracks, flight-paths and shipping-lanes lead to London, directly or indirectly. The visitor to Britain is dumped in the great metropolis before he has scarcely had time to reckon the currency or learn the rudiments of the language from simpler, friendlier folk in the country. Not that the natives of the capital are unfriendly — far from it, they exude that spry cheerfulness which greets all occurrences, civil or uncivil, with a quick volley of humour — but London is predominantly populated by people who are themselves visitors, a myriad of flat-dwellers struggling to grab their chance, involved only in the preoccupations of their own minds and bodies as they plough backwards and forwards between office desks and rented quarters. These people may not know how to show off London at its best to the stranger.

It depends where he wants to begin. According to age, habit or inclination the choice may lie between the traditional, the commercial or the contemporary. The first of these will tackle the monuments to King and Country, God and Justice, and on a fine day these can afford an appropriate grandeur of spectacle for the seeker of history, can elicit admiration or wry smiles from the student of architecture as he takes in the parks with their respective statuary (most remarkable of which, the Albert Memorial), the river with its respective palaces (here embracing the outer reaches of London by including Windsor, Greenwich and Hampton Court), courts of justice, seats of government, victorious warriors in stone, marble, bronze or perched remotely on a column, Tower Bridge,

Marble Arch, Hyde Park Corner, the freedom
of the Mall on days when no traffic is allowed
to interrupt that splendid walk, the chiming bells
of the City churches on a Sunday when that
square mile is emptied like a honeycomb of its
bowler-hatted worker-bees. Curiously, those
seeking the more contemporary pleasures of the
capital gather, at the beginning of their great
adventure, beneath Eros, one of the most
traditional statues. From there they branch out,
in spirit at least, to the caverns and studios
where fashion and music and literature spawn
like multi-coloured mushrooms, which have
helped to give to London once again the
reputation of a great creative centre. On its
streets, from the King's Road to Notting Hill
Gate, the visitor may see and hear the
barometers of taste fluctuate with bewildering
speed.

Between these walks of life, and spanning
the gap like a bridge, is commercial London.
Here the visitor may indulge in the traditional
airs-and-graces of a shopping expedition
(for that is what it must be) through the
courteous West End jungle, or he may venture
to those areas where a good buy usually
involves quick-wittedness and a ready
understanding of the vernacular, the street
markets that are full of surprises.

The past and present Palaces of London, only one of which is occupied by royalty today. Buckingham Palace (*left*), seen from the Mall on the day of the Trooping the Colour ceremony, was purchased from the Duke of Buckingham by George III, rebuilt by George IV, disliked by William IV, and finally occupied by Victoria, for the first time in the capacity of principal royal residence, though it was not until George V that the present facade was added. The Palace of Westminster (*below*) ranks as a palace, being in the charge of the Lord Great Chamberlain, but of its original features only the Great Hall still stands. At Greenwich (*bottom*) the grandiose buildings that represent the Royal Naval College were begun in the image of a palace for Charles II, to succeed the 15th-century Palace of Placentia, so beloved of Tudor sovereigns, which had stood here before, and in which Henry VIII was born and Edward VI died.

The Collegiate Church of St Peter in Westminster, commonly known as Westminster Abbey, probably has more popular history accumulated beneath its splendid roof than any building in the British Isles. Given that every English sovereign, bar two, since Harold has been crowned here and a generous proportion of that number buried, together with poets, soldiers, sailors, statesmen, to each of whom a plinth or slab or altar-tomb, the visitor has a millennium of history to digest before he can in good conscience return to the light of day. Many indeed become so devoted to these studies that they forget to look at the building itself, which is their loss because some of its features beggar all description. Among them is the stupendous grandeur of the nave, the highest Gothic example in England, here offset by the wreaths beneath it, round the tomb of the Unknown Warrior.

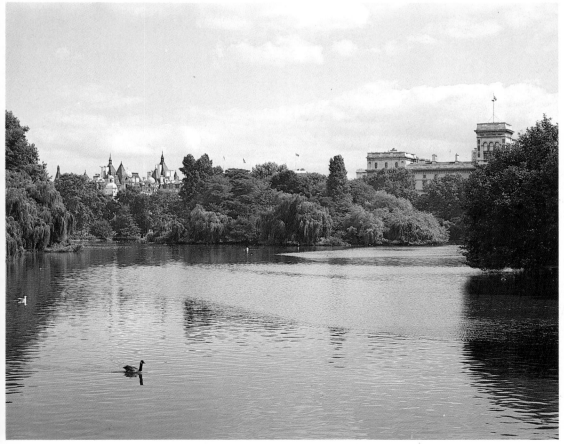

Pageantry, restful scenery and the colourful world of the street market – contrasting aspects of London life. *Above:* stall-holders in the Portobello Road purvey trinkets for the hoarder and charms to catch the acquisitive eye. *Left:* St. James's Park, regarded by many as London's loveliest, provides an oasis of peace and tranquillity for the tourist, office worker and shopper alike. *Far left:* the newly elected Lord Mayor of London arrives in his golden coach at the Law Courts to be presented to the Lord Chancellor.

Fortress, prison, royal palace, the Tower of London's history is more writ in blood than parchment, and no matter how many tourists, cheerful and brightly-dressed, pass through its gates, nothing can expunge those ghosts that haunt its battlements, the presence of those so-called traitors, few of whom deserved the name, who looked, scratched or beat their last upon its walls. Among those murdered, executed, or here condemned to death have been Henry VI, the Duke of Clarence, Edward V, his brother Richard, Anne Boleyn, Thomas More, Catherine Howard, Lady Jane Grey, the Earl of Essex, Sir Walter Raleigh, the Earl of Strafford, Archbishop Laud, the Duke of Monmouth. Among the little pageantries continued today is the Ceremony of the Keys (*below*).

Covent Garden market has been
banished south of the river to
Vauxhall, where it lends its
incomparable blend of crushed fruit
and root crops, delicately touched
with the scent of flowers, to the
Thameside air. The new Covent
Garden, bustling with boutiques and
craft shops, retains much of its old
outer structure. Once they executed
traitors on the site of Smithfield
Market, now they butcher meat –
over 9,000 tons of it is on display for
sale every day in this the largest meat
market in the world. In the early
morning watch the buyers from the
grand hotels prod and argue over the
quality of the fillet.

A bird's-eye view of Hyde Park
Corner, normally one of the busiest
parts of the capital. However, for
once the sun shines, the traffic is
light, the view stretches clear down
Piccadilly, and a string of London
buses parade dutifully for the camera,
nose-to-tail like circus ponies. Until
the last century this was the very
outskirts of London – from here
westwards it was countryside, and
for those who may think the rural
atmosphere has vanished for ever let
them be reassured that behind the
doorway in the south side of
Decimus Burton's Wellington Arch,
or Constitution Hill Arch, is a quite
unbelievably small police-station.

Below left: Tower Bridge, with its distinctive Gothic towers, was built during 1886–94. Its two bascules have been raised to enable ships to pass through – a rare sight nowadays, since shipping in the Thames has considerably declined in recent years.

Below: neatness and formality have been dispensed with in a jumble of signs and occupations, a street of changing names, a cheerful distribution of beers, and the informal gatherings of people in the midday sun. Above pub and telephone booth and office block rises one of the most prominent features of London's skyline, from whose summit this chapter was begun.

Countryside

For the exile returning from abroad, the green of these islands can strike the eye with an almost uncharitable fierceness. Here, the field beside Blea Tarn Farm (Wordsworth's 'one abode, no more') in the Lake District has that brilliant sheen of after-rain, though the above-mentioned poet decided in his time that its colour could be attributed to the hard work of the farmer — 'made green by husbandry of many thrifty years'.
Previous page: an even more variegated collection of greens on the Island of Skye, where the mists regularly sweep down over the peaks of the Cuillins and ensure that the land remains permanently lush. But when the mists lift and the sun breaks through, this island's beauty knows few equals.

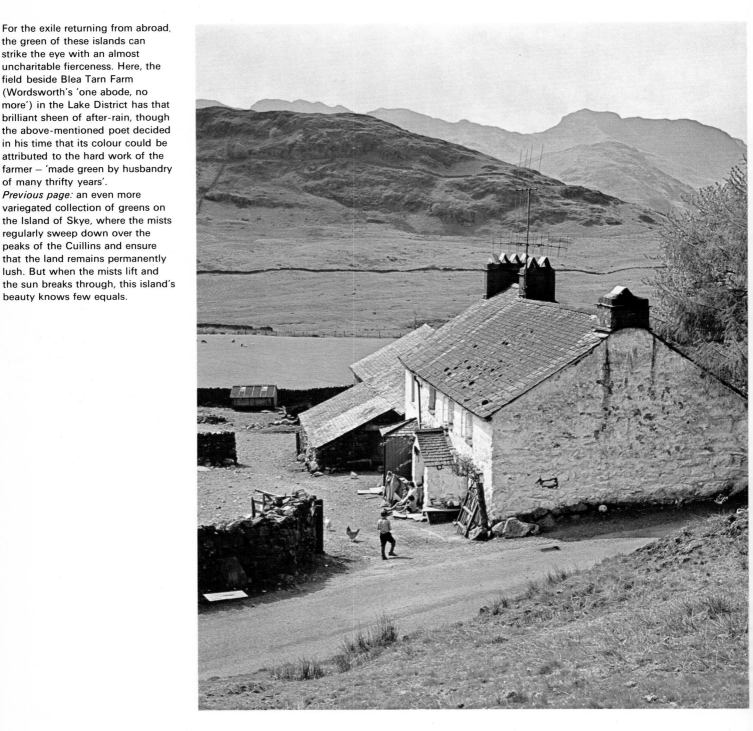

The motorways cross the land, but the land is not dead yet. Let him who thinks the countryside will not surprise him with a fine excess venture into it with all his prejudices bundled in a knapsack and he will see them spilled upon the ground. Lancashire is all industrial towns, he may say, Wales all coal-blackened valleys, East Anglia all marshy fens, and who shall say which will be the greater, his shame when he discovers the untruth of these generalizations or his pleasure at the beauties he did not know were there? Small though the surface area of Britain may be, the unearthing of its various and numberless charms is an age-long process, requiring time, patience with public transport, preferably the initial guidance of one who knows the area, and the will to explore. Unlike many other parts of the world, to drive along the arterial roads of Britain does not, in general, give a fair impression of the nature of the land. Too often the roads demean the landscape instead of becoming platforms for its greater admiration. In other places, of course, they are simply not capable of dealing with the volume of people who rightly wish to enjoy that corner of the country, roads that have not been stretched or straightened since they were first converted from muddy horse-and-carted lanes. In some respects, the railways can give a truer picture, if only because they allow for leisurely inspection of the landscape.

What will he wish to see, this man who explores? Mountains, snowy or craggy, valleys floored by heather or corn, dales that slope away towards hills that buffet the clouds, trim and green Home Counties downs? Will he take the low road that winds to King Arthur's Cornwall, or the high road that snakes across the northern border, up into Scotland, there to seek out the emptiness of the glens, the open stretches of brown turf-sprung moorland where the shaggy sheep stand broadside to the wind and the curlew's cry sounds like melancholy incarnate? Will he cross the Brecons and visit the great glories of Wales, or go beyond to the untethered beauties of the Irish countryside where the hedgerows spill into the roads? Will his restless eye yearn for the level calm of vast East Anglian pastures, or will it search for the plump landscapes of the Weald of Kent? Such are some of the obvious choices; there are less obvious ones which space and time do not allow to be made, and here in this chapter we may only represent a selection of both the well-known and the less-known, beauties acknowledged by generations of travellers and some hitherto unconsidered trifles, those that require the hungrier spirit for their discovery.

For those who weary of formality, be it of life or landscape, there is no finer cure than time spent in the Lake District. Its ruthless and untrammelled countryside revives like no known tonic, arousing in the walker (for that is what any visitor to this area must be), through the rarefied quality of its air, that perfect sense of combined hunger and tiredness which only physical well-being can provide. It may rain for a week, and the clouds may roll inhospitably low over the crags, but the awesomeness of the area will not be diminished. Of course, as the saying goes, on a clear day you can see for ever; witness the pines against the snow at Grisedale (*above*), the long grey road that ribbons away to infinity at the end of Honister Pass (*right*), and the immaculate combination of sun, water, hill and whitewashed houses at Watendlath (*far right*). This last hamlet, by the tarn of the same name, Sir Hugh Walpole used as the principal setting for *Judith Paris* in his 'Herries' saga.

Among the best-known and most impressive crags of the Lake District, the Langdale Pikes seen (*left*) rising above Blea Tarn, and the huge scarred side, like some elderly war-torn elephant, of Great Gable (*above*). Those 'lusty twins', the Langdale Pikes look comparatively benign on this fine autumn day; in brutish weather, especially in the snow, they take on a formidable aspect. By European standards, of course, they are mere pimples — Harrison Stickle, the higher, is 2,401 ft and Pike O'Stickle 2,323 ft but in largely mountainless England they provide a whiff of that particular excitement associated with hills that touch the clouds. Great Gable is some 500 ft higher at 2,949 ft — this view is taken from its neighbour Lingmell — but may still be conquered by the unroped walker.

Windmills with sails intact are rare now; at one time the flat eastern counties of England, just across the North Sea from even flatter Holland, abounded with them, and they could also be seen gracing the skylines of Sussex Downs with their angular scarecrow arms. Some still operate, others are restored to do so, though more often than not the tower is modified to become a 'desirable residence'. The well-preserved specimen on the opposite page is Salvington Mill, near Worthing.

Below: Preston Mill in East Lothian, Scotland, dependant on this stream for its propulsion, has here a delightfully secluded and overgrown air. So, too, has the water in front of the handsome whitewashed farm (*right*) near Kirkbean, Kirkcudbrightshire, in the south-west Lowlands. But let those who may scorn the Solway Firth as being of intemperate climate look now upon this scene, almost Mediterranean in its assembled brilliance.

Eden Valley in the Pennines,
well-named with its patchwork of
rich broad acres beneath a fine
expanse of sky. But it has its
serpent too, a devil much embraced
by local superstition, the Helm
Wind. No imaginary creature this, it
sweeps in violent icy blasts down
across the dales, and in the spring
may blow for a fortnight without
respite. It is at this time of year that
you may see the farmers with their
eyes fixed on the cloud formations,
for it is a particular gathering of
clouds over the hills that signals
the approaching onslaught of the
Helm. And, for the farmers,
onslaught is the word — crops have
been swept away, fences blown
down, cows and sheep tumbled
down hills or buried in snow-drifts
on the fell-sides, and bunches of
hay have been seen careering
across the sky, hundreds of feet up,
like a squadron of witches.

The inner countryside that soothes, 'balm of hurt minds'. Shakespeare used the quotation differently but he was not to know the shock of pleasure that today's harassed city-dweller finds in such retreats — lanes unpolluted except by the farm tractor, cold clear light through silver birch trees onto that dense silence of ferns, the marvellous oppression of a day of fat summer when the hedgerows invade the path and long grasses reach out to be plucked and chewed.

Not until some fine surprising day in March do you feel the weight of winter lifted from the back of the land. Then, though the frosts may yet return and the month go out like a roaring lion, you are entitled to acknowledge that the days of fires, and overcoats, and dankness in the lungs, are numbered. The sunlit beech trees bordering the ploughed field are here caught on such a day of spring.

The summer has its weight too (*right*), the days of heat when the cumulus builds up around the edge of the sky into towering castles of wool and the air is heavy like a blanket. Suddenly the storm breaks, and with the rain the earth and air shuffle off their deadness like a snake its skin.

A remarkable Gothic scene, snow in the gulleys and storm clouds above, the last burst of evening sunlight turning the landscape a rancid gold as if signalling its readiness for sacrifice to the elements. All that it lacks is the accompanying soundtrack of horses' hooves and rattling carriage, the heroine fleeing to her lover . . .

No such lunacy affects the sequestered intimacy of these spring saplings (*inset*); even the photograph seems an intrusion on the private world of some unseen *Wind in the Willows* character.

A. E. Housman wrote of the 'coloured counties', and from Clee Hill in Shropshire (*top left*) you do have that impression of the quilt of England laid before your feet. Away to the west is the border with Wales, still echoing with the skirmishes that inflamed the Marches, the feuds that severed Saxon from Celt.

Such magnificent panoramas are found but rarely in the south of England, as indeed are hills that are both reasonably high and readily accessible, which probably explains why both Box Hill and Leith Hill, near Dorking in Surrey, attract visitors like a magnet. The scarred appearance of Box Hill (*below left*) bears witness to the thousands who have slithered, slipped, rolled or tobogganed down its satisfying slopes.

Below: A fine view across the water, and a fine feed for the gulls, as the plough turns over virgin earth near Loch Dunvegan on the Isle of Skye.

There is not much to be said about the Mountains of Mourne (*left below*) that hasn't been better sung. They do sweep down to the sea, and are by general consent the most beautiful range in Northern Ireland. Stretching from Newcastle to Newry, they produce a dozen peaks above 2,000 ft, the highest being Slieve Donard which overlooks Newcastle and from its summit possesses magnificent views clear across to the Isle of Man.

Below: looking up towards the Black Mountains from the market town of Crickhowell in the lovely valley of the Usk, Powys.

Over the other side is the English border, and at Crickhowell are the ruins of a 13th-century castle, one of a long line of strongholds in the Usk lowlands. Romans, Normans, Saxons have tramped these hills on missions of unholy war against the Welsh.

Mountains, moors and glens of darker aspect, the face of war, the long red thread in the tribal memory. This last will never be lifted from the name of Glencoe (*far right, top*), the 'Glen of Weeping', chosen, you might think, deliberately for its mournful dramatic impact by Campbell of Glenlyon when he set out to massacre forty Macdonalds in their beds. The clouds, the mists, the towering walls of rock combine to preserve the melancholy of that time.

The Romans fought to preserve what they had conquered; with a kind of crazed defiance they built a wall, seventy-three miles of it, across the top of England (*right*) to ward off the Celts. We may be grateful for the greatest surviving monument of their occupation, but how they must have suffered, those centurions from the warm south manning these frozen ramparts on the Northumberland moors. For 250 years they garrisoned it, with nothing to enjoy except the view. *Below right:* the forest of Mamlorn, Breadalbane, Perthshire, has not such an immediate place in the history books, but its setting has a theatrical beauty, especially at that time of winter when the Grampians are snow-capped.

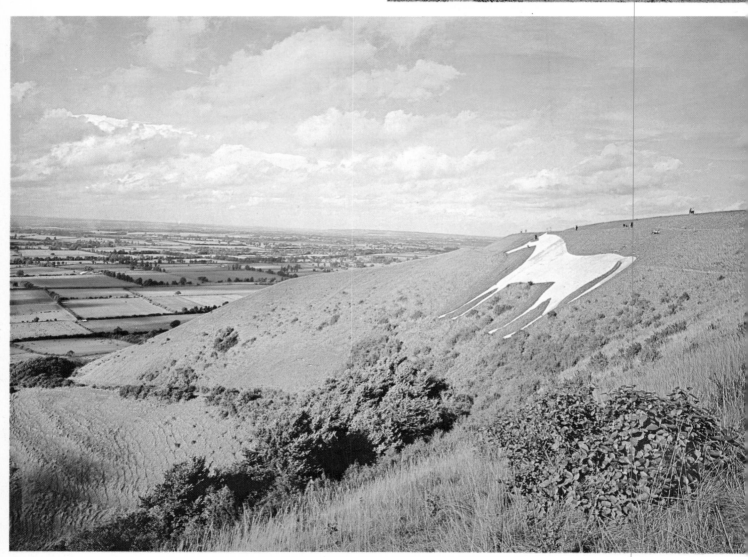

Visible from the Cotswolds and from the Welsh hills, and rising splendidly above the broad valley of the River Severn, the Malvern Hills (*left*) run for nine miles along the border between the old counties of Worcestershire and Herefordshire, attaining nearly 1,400 ft at the highest point, from where the view stretches to embrace several counties, including the six battlefields of Worcester, Tewkesbury, Evesham, Shrewsbury, Edgehill and Mortimer's Cross. *Below left:* the White Horse of Westbury, one of the many White Horses cut in the chalky Wiltshire escarpment. This one, known to be of ancient, possibly Iron Age,

origin was remodelled in the 18th century; and today the picnickers, with scant respect for history, unfold their baskets in its grassy eye.
Below: Symond's Yat, Hereford and Worcester, where the Wye twists through a gorge ('yat' means gate or pass). Famous as a beauty spot, it too commands spectacular views.

Monuments

'Half church of God, half castle 'gainst the Scot.' So Sir Walter Scott wrote of Durham, and the inscription may be read on the bridge beneath the towering Cathedral. Most of the great buildings of this land have their inscriptions or their epitaphs, have been instruments of history or dramatic props of literature, and monuments — with its dictionary definition of 'anything that preserves the memory of a person or an event, a building, pillar, tomb, tablet, statue etc; any structure, natural or artificial, considered as an object of beauty or of interest as a relic of the past; a notable or enduring example' — seems to be the noun appropriate to embrace the collective virtues of castles, cathedrals, country houses, abbeys, stone circles and so forth, which are here gathered in this chapter. Again some of them have stones that seep familiar history, others have walls which were only stormed in feuds of a more regional nature. The castles of Britain are worthy of anyone's study, but the pity of it is that so many have been left to fall into disrepair, abandoned to mouldering ruins either when the owner-family was besieged and uprooted, or when economics dictated that they could no longer be supported, or maybe (fancifully) when their history became too ghastly for their continued habitation and only ravens could abide the battlements which rang with the ghostly shrieks of tortured kings, the torments of Richard, Edward, false fleeting perjur'd royalty. Country houses, on the other hand, tend to have more sedate histories, built to ennoble the landscape as well as the life-style of their occupiers and

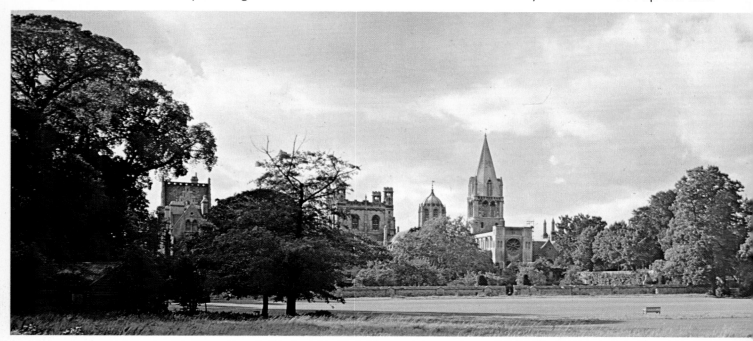

as such are frequently preserved together with their huge well-cultivated gardens.

The visitor to Britain could do worse, if time restricted him, than travel to each of the cathedrals. In so doing he would see the cities and, in between, criss-cross the countryside. And no two cathedrals are alike — the experience of being in the presence of great architecture will each time produce a whole complex of emotions, each time differing in intensity according to the effect of that particular building. Great echoing naves with vaulted roofs, saints and soldiers flattened with hands clasped above their tombs, windows that sometimes seem created, as do the cathedrals themselves, beyond the call of duty, faith, mortal endeavour. The abbeys too have their greatness, and not a little sadness. Usually more inaccessible than the cathedrals, and deliberately so, their lovely ruined arches seem to mock today's pedestrian efforts at grandeur in concrete. Finally, and not least, the visitor may wish to see one of the many groups of ancient stones that stand about the country — genuine monuments to a distant and only partially understood past.

No contrast could be more pronounced than that between the fiery sunset over Castle Stalker and Loch Linnhe in Argyll (*previous page*) and the late summer sun on Christ Church Meadows, Oxford. Castle Stalker, silhouetted on its island rock like something out of a fairy tale, was built by Duncan Stewart of Appin in the reign of James IV, subsequently lost to its owner as the result of a wager, and is now a ruin. Christ Church has seen its share of eccentric bets, but none that actually involved the disposal of the buildings. Founded by Cardinal Wolsey it houses the Cathedral church of Oxford, has numbered the creator of Alice in Wonderland among its academics and a succession of Prime Ministers-to-be among its pupils. One of its further claims to fame, Wren's Tom Tower, may be glimpsed on this skyline of spires, between the Cathedral and the Hall.

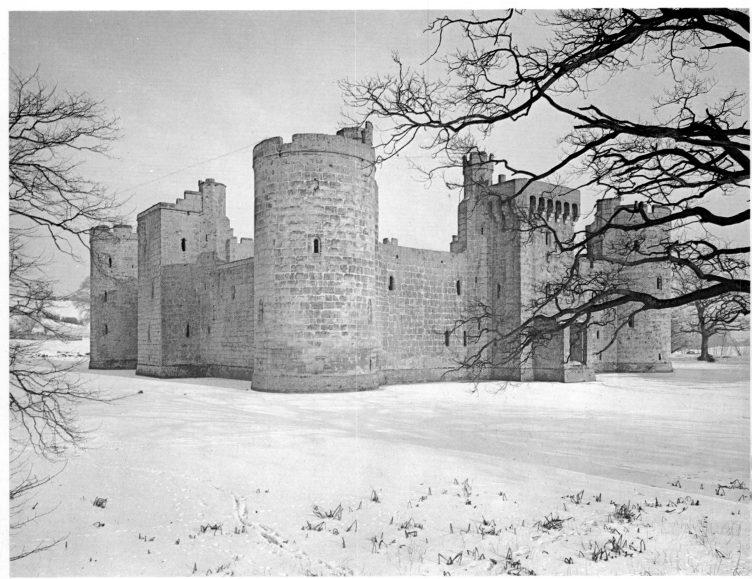

Left: two fortresses, strong both against invasion. Tantallon Castle and beyond, at the mouth of the Firth of Forth, the Bass Rock. The latter used to house a castle, at one time a grim prison for Covenanters, but it was destroyed in 1694. Tantallon was the seat of the for-ever-feuding Douglases, and resisted all attempts at capture until General Monk bombarded it for twelve days in 1651. The building has been in decay since the end of that century when the Douglases sold it.

Below left: Bodiam Castle, Sussex, on the other hand, never ever suffered an attack and thus remains an almost perfectly preserved example of 14th-century castle architecture, standing out above its frozen snow-covered moat like every child's idea of a medieval fort.

Below: for a thousand years the citizens of Edinburgh have been able to see their castle from every quarter of the town, rising a clear 450 ft above sea-level, the sheer wall on one side scaled only thrice in all that time. Capital castle in the capital city of Scotland, it has lost none of its imposing grandeur in this belittling age.

Sunlight on broken columns; arches tall, squat, delicate, and ornate; immaculate silence save for the wind flicking through hollow windows and the sudden jabbering of birds who have made their nest in a cloistered corner. The Abbeys of Britain are mostly ruins now, a fact which for some enhances their virtues of contemplative quiet and points up the noble patterns of their architecture.

Above: Crowland Abbey, Lincolnshire, built in the 8th century, burnt three times and shaken once by earthquake, now has only the North aisle and the tower surviving and this is used as a parish church.

Above right: Cleeve Abbey, Avon, a late 12th-century foundation for Cistercian monks, has an excellently preserved refectory (reconstructed in the 15th century) and generally well-preserved convent buildings but the church is in ruins.

Far right: Melrose Abbey, Roxburghshire, 12th-century Cistercian also, and once one of the richest abbeys in Scotland, is far more extensive than this picture

indicates, and among its hidden treasures is the heart of Robert the Bruce, supposedly buried beneath the East window.

Right: fair Fountains Abbey in North Yorkshire, founded 1132, burnt, rebuilt, sacked by Henry VIII, and now among the most beautiful ruins in the country, seemingly grown in stature since its roof was dismantled and its wealth scattered.

A Border bastion, Caerlaverock Castle, Dumfriesshire (*above*), crumbling in its moat. Built in 1290 (though later much altered and added to), it changed hands between English and Scots like a bad penny, finally capitulating to the Covenanters in 1640 and thereafter being left to the elements. It has passed into literature as the 'Ellangowan' of Scott's *Guy Mannering*.

Right: the tattered ramparts of Corfe. Uneasy have lain the heads that wore the Crown inside this Dorset castle. In 978 the young King Edward was murdered by his stepmother, Queen Elfrida, at the gate of the Saxon stronghold that preceded the present Norman buildings; it was a favourite royal residence of King John; and poor Edward II was incarcerated here before being dragged away to his hideous death in Berkeley Castle. Finally it was defended for King Charles by Lady Bankes, gallantly resisting the onslaught of 600 Parliamentary troops until by treachery they seized it and by gunpowder reduced it.

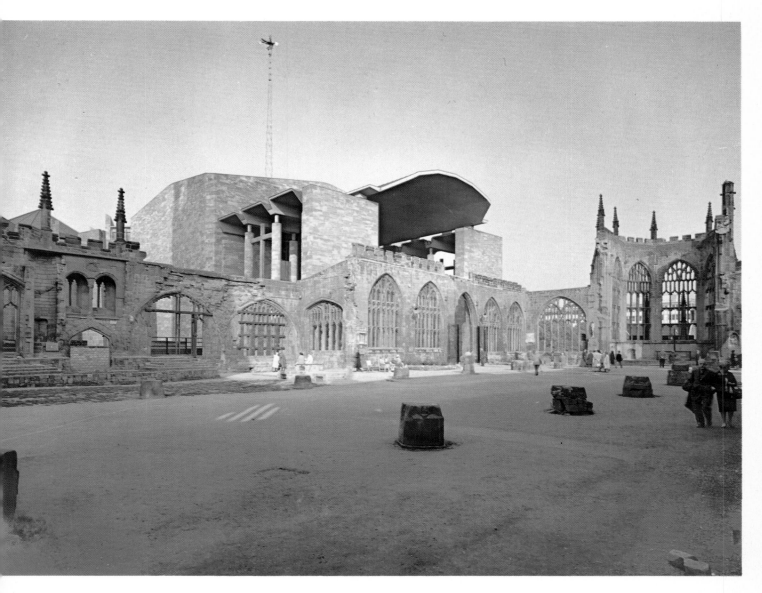

Left: Bath has given its name to buns, biscuits, chaps and chairs, it has been called the 'Florence of England', and in its time the pens of Dickens, Sheridan, Smollett, Thackeray, Fielding, Fanny Burney and of course Jane Austen have done their literary best for it. Roman legions and Regency bucks have delighted in its charms and sampled its waters for their aches and pains.

By contrast until recent years, Coventry's fame rested principally on cloth, cycles, cars, the long blond tresses of one Lady Godiva, and a magnificent Gothic cathedral.

The cities share a common experience. Bath, in no way a target for war, was nevertheless wantonly bombed in 1942 and had to be extensively rebuilt, while Coventry, on the night of 14 November 1940, suffered the most appalling blitz ever experienced by a British city. As a result a whole new city was built in the ruins of the old, becoming in the process a landmark of urban redevelopment. Crowning this is the new Cathedral, rising above and alongside the hollow shell of its razed predecessor (*above*).

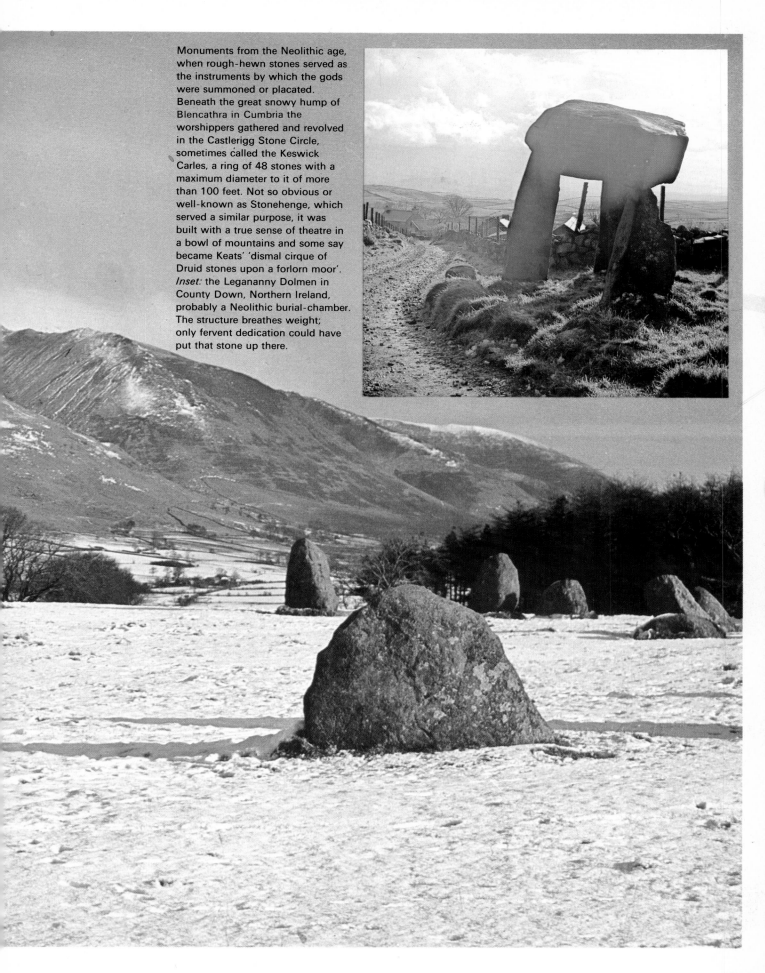

Monuments from the Neolithic age, when rough-hewn stones served as the instruments by which the gods were summoned or placated. Beneath the great snowy hump of Blencathra in Cumbria the worshippers gathered and revolved in the Castlerigg Stone Circle, sometimes called the Keswick Carles, a ring of 48 stones with a maximum diameter to it of more than 100 feet. Not so obvious or well-known as Stonehenge, which served a similar purpose, it was built with a true sense of theatre in a bowl of mountains and some say became Keats' 'dismal cirque of Druid stones upon a forlorn moor'. *Inset:* the Legananny Dolmen in County Down, Northern Ireland, probably a Neolithic burial-chamber. The structure breathes weight; only fervent dedication could have put that stone up there.

Three of the stately temples that still grace this land, to man, God, or *folie de grandeur*. Blenheim Palace (*bottom left*) has probably more of the last, donated by a grateful Queen Anne to John Churchill, 1st Duke of Marlborough, for his string of victories in the Low Countries, especially the one from

which the vast mansion takes its name. The unfinished masterpiece of Vanbrugh, it also owes its glories to many other distinguished craftsmen, and it renewed its prominence in the history books by being the birthplace of Sir Winston Churchill.
Montacute House, Somerset

(*above*) seems to have all that was best of the Elizabethan age. Generous without being vulgar, formal without being severe, it is worthy of long pilgrimage.
Above left: the longest cathedral in Europe, majestic square-towered Winchester has seen kings crowned and buried, homage paid and

ecclesiastical decree proclaimed over the centuries in which its city has been sometime joint-capital of the land and its college the cradle of aspiring scholarship.

Villages and Country Towns

The villages and country towns of Britain,
the obvious beauties of the land, tend to be
the parts of the country that get spoiled in the
mind's eye by over-emphasis, by over-exposure
perhaps in the cinema travelogue or by the
too heavy tread of sentiment when thought
about in absence. Not that they are ever
spoiled in themselves — nothing short of nuclear
holocaust could do that, and it is perhaps
allowable for yet another voice to rise in praise
of their virtues. In this chapter, as indeed
throughout the book, the aim has been to
show the beautiful well-known with the
beautiful less-known, thereby affording a
broader vision of the countryside than a mere
assembly of picture postcards of famous views
could give. Those places that are familiar may
therefore be recognized with nostalgia by those
who have fleetingly visited them, and those
places that seem strange may hopefully either
be sought out or here acknowledged for their
charms. The choice was infinite — in every
county is a village that might be described as
'typical', in every village a scene that qualifies
as 'picturesque'. But what is 'typical'?
Cornish whitewashed houses on a steep road
that leads down to the sea, the warm brown
stone of Cotswold villages, rose-covered
cottages in Kent, tiny houses buried in the
Berkshire downs, the timber-frames of Suffolk,
the simple frontage of a row of Lakeland
dwellings — all these may be said to represent
the typical, but they are typical only of the
area they occupy and in which they are the
predominant feature, and that area can be very
small. To say they are typical of Britain is only

true insofar as they are not typical of France, or Norway, or Nigeria, because not found there. But within Britain to say one is typical is to say that all are, and many more for whom there is no room upon these pages.

One feature, though, which cannot escape notice and of which all visitors from abroad demand the experience — the English pub. To a few it is an over-rated institution, to most the very backbone of our country life, almost the local parliament, where reputations may be lost and won in an evening, yarns of immense length and increasing fiction spun for hours on end, boasts roared, threats taunted, quarrels mended and marriages sealed. 'I do but play with an imagined life,' wrote Browning, thinking of something else, but it is a fair bet that most Englishmen caught up in circumstances that separate them from home — war, foreign service, etc — do play at some time or another with an imagined life that centres round the bar, and the company, of a pub they have known in the country.

Like the country girl who becomes a film star overnight, and lives to regret her inability ever to return to the simple unfettered life, Castle Combe was swept to fame a few years back by being elected Prettiest Village in England and since then has struggled against the tide of invaders bent on confirming for themselves the rightness of this decision. The Hollywood moguls were among them, and it is a tribute to the enduring quality of this Wiltshire village that its charms remain untarnished.
Previous page: there are many Cornish villages that share the features of Boscastle, with its prominence of slate, the liberal laying-on of whitewash, the steep and narrow road that leads down to the sea. The nearby slate quarries of Delabole were in fact the original reason for Boscastle's existence, for its tiny harbour, overshadowed by precipitous cliffs, was built for the export of the slate.

There are many, among them some of the greatest landscape painters this country has known, who have sworn that the beauties of East Anglia are without peer. Others, more used to the cosy proximity of hills, will argue that those endless sweeps of pancake-flat terrain, the marshes, heaths and vast acreages of corn are an acquired taste. Never acquired unless attempted, and the novitiate could do worse than aim for these two handsome representatives for a start. Norwich, the capital of Norfolk, with castle, cathedral and, lately, university, has all the finest qualities of a provincial city—activity, spaciousness, generosity of spirit. Elm Hill (*left*), with its cobbles and overhangs, is among the best preserved of its streets.

Suffolk's Lavenham (*above*) thrives on preservation. A small 15th-century town that prospered in the wool trade, fostered by those huge East Anglian pastures, it has determinedly kept what it has won, in particular a predominance of magnificent timber-framed houses. Among them are the famous Guildhall and Wool Hall, and several which lean drunkenly one way or another, chief of these being the Crooked House pictured above.

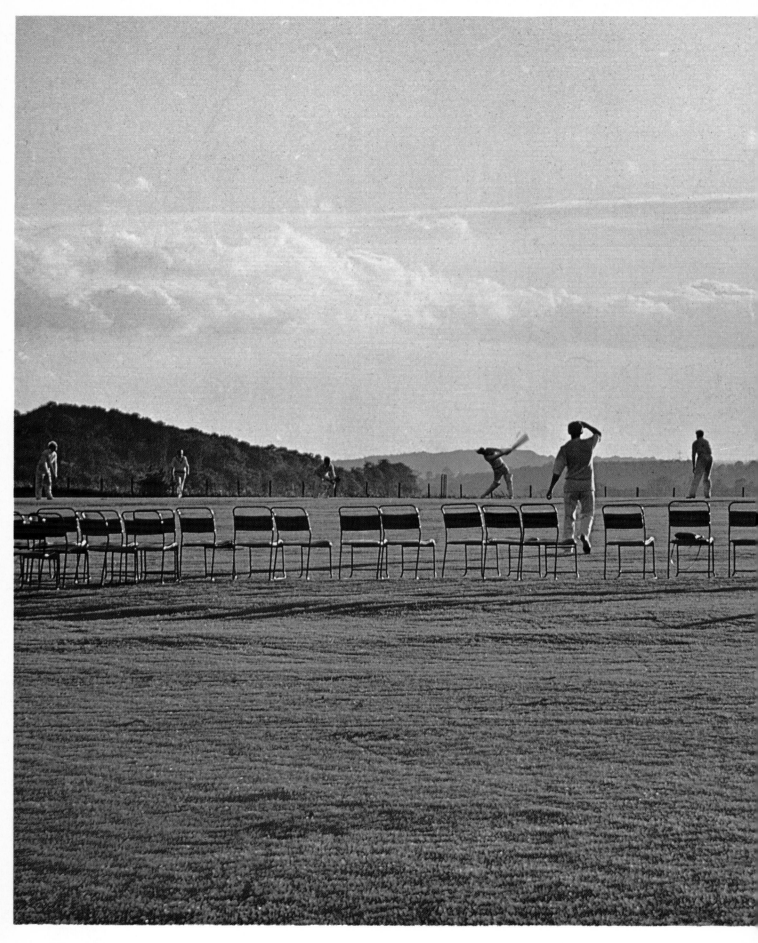

A line of empty seats, but a few spectators who still appreciate the grace and subtleties of cricket, the game the foolish say will die but which in fact has its roots buried deep in a country tradition — wherever a few level acres of grass may be found with a pub adjacent. Most would probably agree that the true nature of the game, its style and delicate sense of theatre, is best transmitted on summer evenings such as this when thirst lengthens with the shadows. They certainly know it at Hambledon, as they did two hundred years ago when the game is said to have been born here, to which fact a memorial stands witness on Broadhalfpenny Down opposite the Bat and Ball Inn.

Discovered country to whose bourn the travellers return, the England that fills postcards and home-thoughts-from-abroad — ye olde inn, a jar of ale, thatched cottages swathed in the thick scarf of summer.

The small octagonal-shaped inn at St Albans (*top*), the Fighting Cocks, bears the legend that it is the oldest inhabited licensed house in England, while the Masons Arms (*above*) at Branscombe in South Devon can certainly lay claim to being one of the best examples of the genre. In a delightful village, sheltered by hills on either side and reached by steep and twisting lanes, the pub is within a few minutes walk of the sea across the fields.

Right: Welford-on-Avon, Warwickshire, a view that summons up the charm and innocence of a long-lost childhood when all the world was summer.

'There live not three good men unhanged in England, and one of them is fat and grows old'. In fact Falstaff sits and grows old in stately bronze, holding court to the populace who visit his creator's native Stratford, the town which bore him, bred him, and finally, when the whirligig of time brought in its revenges, buried him. This last was done in Holy Trinity Church (*left*), beside the Avon, and the stone slab therein, together with the monuments of his life and the theatre which re-creates his plays, is one of the much-visited spots.

Above: another poet is connected with this place, Hawkshead in Cumbria near Coniston Water. Wordsworth attended the Grammar school and his name may be seen carved on one of the desks. He would no doubt have been aware of the 15th-century monastic court house pictured above, formerly the the property of Furness Abbey, and where once, in Falstaff's terms, the 'rusty curb of old father antic the law' could be heard and seen at work.

Three places all acknowledged for their fairness. Broadway (*above*) in Hereford and Worcester is by popular consent the finest Cotswold village, though popular consent may have damaged its appeal. Antique dealers and motor-cars now provide opulent distraction in the broad main street, deserted here in this picture which shows to good effect the famous local Cotswold stone gleaming in a stormy light.

Bath (*below right*) has had its classical and 18th-century praises sung unstintingly, and perhaps these are most warmly felt today by a population who can enjoy colonnaded walks where they may shop away from traffic. And what could be finer on a sunlit morning than this prospect of the Abbey seen beyond baskets of flowers in full bloom?

Above right: the village is well-known even if the garden is not, but the garden ought to be, as an example of English horticultural pride and care. The garden is in the Cambridgeshire village of Hemingford Grey, which has a reputation both for being pretty and for containing what is possibly the oldest-inhabited house in England.

Below: these thatched cottages at Selworthy in Somerset are perhaps representative of what is best known and most photographed in the English countryside. Trim and unpretentious, they have been preserved through the generations by diligent re-applications of whitewash, and their ordered calm contrasts well with the haphazard profusion of trees behind them.

Such scenes are often to be found in Somerset — villages clutched in hollows while from above the view opens out across the valley to wooded hills beyond. From the churchyard just above these cottages, for instance, there is a magnificent prospect of distant Dunkery Beacon.

Right: Tintagel's history is long on legend, most of it connected with King Arthur, and visitors to this Cornish village rush to see the crumbling romantic ruins of its castle, which seems to ooze eventful past. In so doing it is easy to pass by the Old Post Office, pictured here, so called because it was a letter-receiving office in the second half of the 19th century but which in fact was built to the plan of a manor house in the 14th century, probably only two centuries after the castle.

As far as is known, no curfew prevails in Hutton-le-Hole in North Yorkshire (*left*), nor apparently has the village been deserted on the grounds of fire, famine or pestilence. Perhaps some deep sense of Yorkshire thrift has locked the inhabitants inside; more probably it is the early hours of daylight and they sleep in honest beds. The photographer is abroad before even the milk churns are collected, aware of the photogenic possibilities of these interesting configurations of white painted posts.

Above: Not a mouse stirs in Pluckley either, in the Weald of Kent, but an imaginative hand has been at work converting this oast-house and zebra-striped barn into an eminently habitable home.

'The web of our life is of a mingled yarn, good and ill together.' In Shakespeare's time two of the places pictured here would have been important centres for that mingled yarn from which he drew his metaphor. Kersey (*far right*) built a sound prosperity on the Suffolk sheep, and gave its name to a cloth, while pride of place in Dunster, Somerset (*right*) still belongs to the Old Yarn Market, which dates from about 1600. Kersey, like Lavenham, is still unspoiled, and one of its incidental charms is the water-splash in the main street.

Below: '. . . good and ill together.' The clouds move on out over the Solway Firth, leaving puddles, mud, and watery light slanting across this attractive row of houses in Allonby, Cumbria.

In many of the country towns of Britain history can be dug up like truffles, odd corners made more interesting by the discovery of some obliging curiosity. Both Rye (*above*) in Sussex, and Cirencester (*left*) in Gloucestershire can be rich providers of such fare, having both an extensive and noteworthy past. Rye, sometime Cinque Port and smuggling haunt, has been burned down twice by the French, has seen its surrounding countryside submerged by the sea and has been the home of Henry James. Cirencester, *Corinium* to the Romans and built by them to be the second city of Britain, was destroyed by the Saxons, invaded by the Normans and subsequently restored to be a thriving market town. Both towns have, however, a curiosity in common in these pictures. Cirencester Parish Church is one of the largest in England, and one of the most beautiful examples of Perpendicular, an unusual feature being the elaborate three-storey South porch. The Church of St Mary in Rye, on the other hand, has a clock which dates back to the 16th century and is believed to be the oldest in England still functioning with its original mechanism.

Inland Waters

How many would choose to live by one or other of these islands' waters if they were given the opportunity? This book began with the sea, which has been so much fortress, protector and benefactor; it ends with the inland waters of Britain which, for many, represent a haven and an ideal. Some worship the great rivers, Thames and Severn, Avon, Tees and Tyne, the 'smug and silver Trent', which trace like veins of mercury across the land; worship them for their traffic or their powers of commerce, for their strength which turns water mills or pumps electricity, but more likely, far inland, for their sweetness which carries them, the worshippers, along their watery backs in cabin cruiser, yacht, dinghy or canoe, from county to county taking days on end to accomplish what the aggressive motor-car will achieve in hours.

Others find Nirvana in the lakes, or lochs, or loughs, cradles of legend, of monsters (real or imagined?), giant puddles in the mountains from which they take their strength and depth. Here are the waters, brimming, bright and large, upon which the fisherman pushes out his boat and sits in undistracted solitude, far out in the silence while the white mists gather over his head like a wraith. And here, too, the sudden squalls blow up, pummelling the surface and pounding the waves like creamy fists through the reeds at the water's edge. The fisherman who seeks a louder setting will stand in the raging shallows of a river, casting for the fish that fight upstream against the current, listening to the thunder as the torrent splits its streams between the boulders, tumbles,

splits again, falls precipitate, and then regathers in a foaming cauldron at the base.

There are surely many who would like to live within sight and sound of water, even if it be only a wee burn rippling at the bottom of the garden. Nor is such a desire solely the prerogative of the romantic spirit. In this day and age, when the roar of traffic encroaches more and more upon the daily lives of thousands, when the eardrums are penetrated by the most continuously unmusical sound that man has yet invented, it is no more than a sensible concern for physical and mental health which seeks to replace it with the rhythm of falling waters, no matter how furious or torrential. And for the eye, water, still or moving, and nearly always it is moving, however imperceptibly, is perhaps the most intensely watchable phenomenon of all. It is to be hoped that this chapter will not create the impression of Britain as a land overflowing with rivers and lakes, a giant marsh of a country, for that would be untrue. These watery pictures are meant as an unspoken reassurance of the landscape's sanity, of what we may in troubled times consider as a longed-for refuge.

Ullswater, glimpsed (*below*) through trees on a windy autumn day, and (*above*) nailed by winter, flotsam tethered in jagged ice. This unusual effect was obtained by the lake freezing, then thawing, and the wind blowing the ice-floes to the shore, where they were gripped by another severe freeze.
Previous page: Derwentwater, crowned by the cold peak of Skiddaw and, with its withered reeds, looking like the setting for Keats' *La Belle Dame Sans Merci*. If you can bear the low temperatures a visit to the Lake District in the dead of winter can sometimes be more visually satisfying than at other times of the year.

Above: Buttermere and its neighbour Crummock Water seen from Fleetwith Pike—a sense of splendid isolation, of magic lakes viewed from a dragon's lair as he guards the entrance to the pass. To come back to reality, these two lakes were once one, and it can be clearly seen how they were cut in two, divided by the detritus brought down by mountain streams. Unless it be thought the Lake District is all barren crag and unpeopled pasture, let the eye feast on the views of Grasmere and Dunmail Raise (*left*) from the fells near Red Bank. Many will know that Wordsworth, that master of solitude, chose the community of Grasmere as his home for ten years, close by the nearly circular lake of the same name with the island in the middle, and it would be a stony heart that did not think he chose wisely.

Monuments to vaulting ambition, accomplished in different shapes and sizes. *Right:* the Clifton Suspension Bridge, one of the massive achievements (though not completed until after his death) of the great Isambard Kingdom Brunel, among other things engineer of the Great Western Railway and builder of the Great Western and Great Eastern Steamships. Begun in 1831, and incorporating suspension chains from Brunel's Hungerford Bridge, which was being demolished, it fills the sky 245 feet above the Avon Gorge. Older and more modest in proportions is the Clapper Bridge (*above*), built long ago out of slabs of stone. This particular one is near Great Asby in Cumbria, but they are most frequently found in Devon.

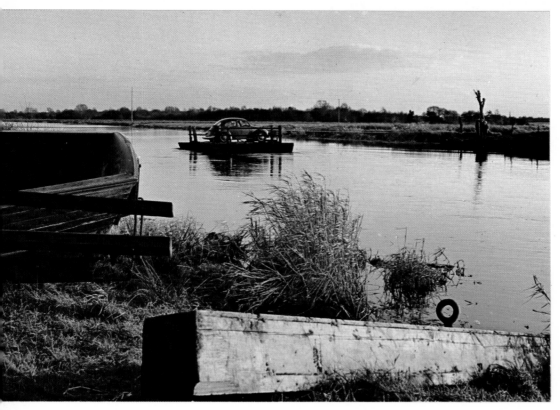

The soothing presence of water —
in these frenetic times perhaps of
more emotional benefit than
practical. Under graceful
Flemish-style bridges and flanked
by lawns, the River Windrush
runs parallel to the main street in
the Cotswold village of
Bourton-on-the-Water (*far left*).
A further attraction here is a
sizeable model of the village made
out of the local stone.
Top left: a leisurely unsophisticated
method of transporting a car across
water via the Bann ferry at the
entrance to Lough Neagh in
Northern Ireland. This picture gives
no indication that the lough is in
fact by some considerable distance
the largest lake in the British Isles.
Eighteen miles long, eleven miles
wide, ten rivers flow into it and
five counties share its shores.
Below left: the sunlit steeple and
the stacked houses of Ross-on-Wye
above its curving river in that
corner of England which numbers
among the most cherished beauties
of these islands.

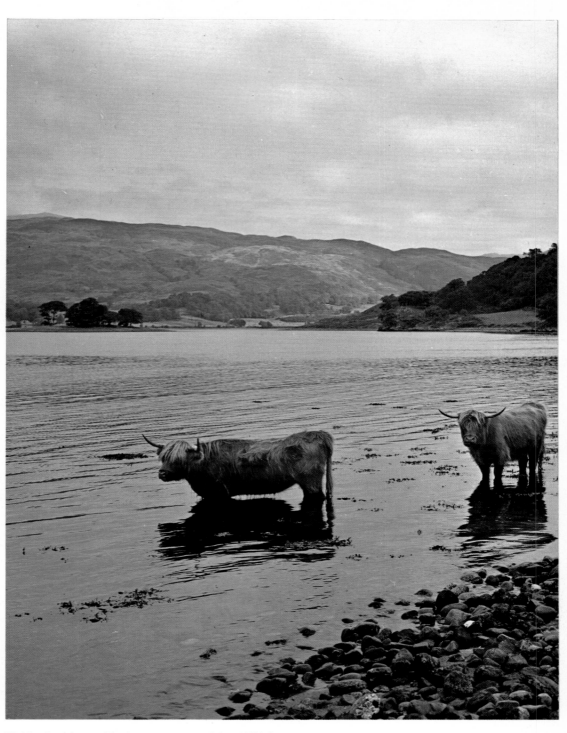

Highland cattle stand in the shallows of Loch Etive (*above*) in Argyllshire, a great sea loch with a variety of wild scenery converging on its shores in its eighteen miles of length — woods, mountains, empty echoing glens, and at its mouth the Falls of Lora, the sea-rapids that cascade over a reef of rocks and whose music Ossian heard and made famous. These are now crossed by an impressive cantilever bridge.

Left: smaller but not less imposing, Llyn Gwynant in Gwynedd can be seen in its entirety, encircled by traditional Welsh scenery — acres of sheep pasture and the musical mountains that have sired all those poets with the dancing rain in their voices.

No savage splendour to these waters, only the continuous rubbing on the stone-cast of walls, the quick rippling of the surface as the breeze flicks it. The water that surrounds Ightham Mote (*far left*) is fresh from a spring, a natural moat to this handsome Kent manor house that was built in the 14th century, added to in the 15th, and has been occupied virtually without break since then.

Left: a ferry crosses the River Avon to this landing-stage at Fladbury in Hereford and Worcester, though it is out of sight here, moored in the water-lilies along this bank and no doubt becalmed under the flat blade of indolent midsummer.

The much-loved and oft-frequented waters of East Anglia. *Left:* a convenient mooring on a bend of the River Bure at Coltishall on the Norfolk Broads, those waters that cover thousands of acres and which hordes of landlubbers take to navigating for their summer holidays, crazily tacking between the many attractive pubs that come down to the rivers' edge. The true nature of the Broads is best seen at those times of year when the wild life predominates, when in the reeds and marshes and shallows may be heard the frenzied orchestrations of a great variety of birds, some of them not commonly found elsewhere in England. *Above:* the Stour in Suffolk may not suffer the boating invasion of the Norfolk Broads but many thousands of eyes have feasted on it indirectly, through the works of Constable. He once said that he associated his 'careless boyhood with all that lies on the banks of the Stour; those scenes made me a painter'. Here is a stretch of that river, at Flatford, that must have seemed a paradise to a small boy with its secretive air.

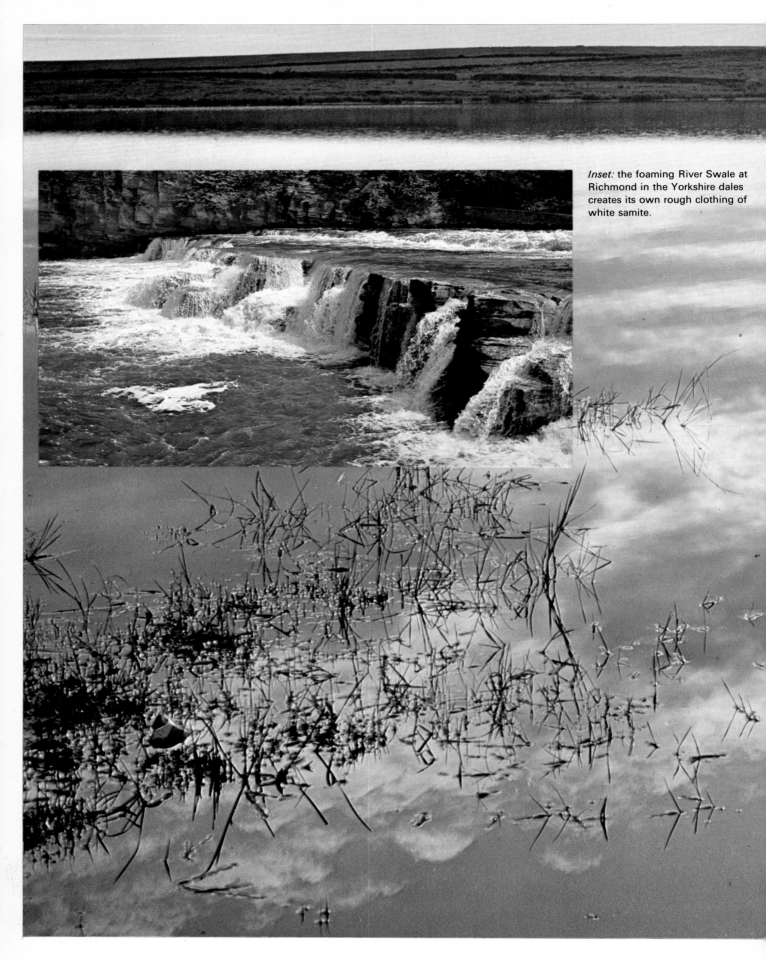

Inset: the foaming River Swale at Richmond in the Yorkshire dales creates its own rough clothing of white samite.

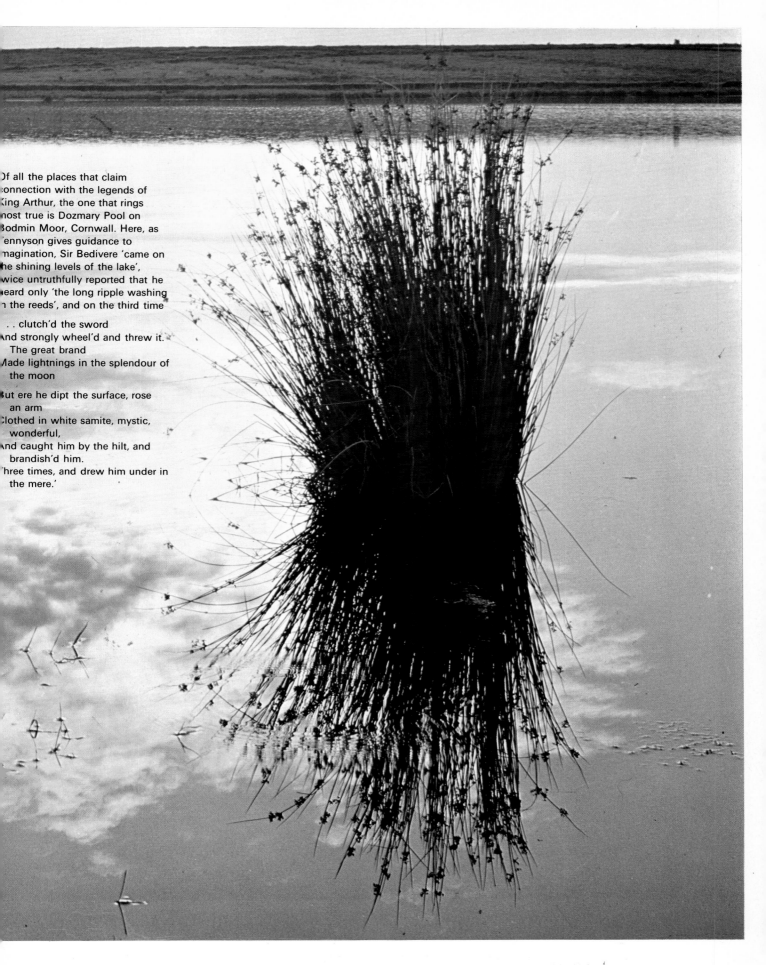

Of all the places that claim
connection with the legends of
King Arthur, the one that rings
most true is Dozmary Pool on
Bodmin Moor, Cornwall. Here, as
Tennyson gives guidance to
imagination, Sir Bedivere 'came on
the shining levels of the lake',
twice untruthfully reported that he
heard only 'the long ripple washing
in the reeds', and on the third time

. . . clutch'd the sword
And strongly wheel'd and threw it.
    The great brand
Made lightnings in the splendour of
    the moon

But ere he dipt the surface, rose
    an arm
Clothed in white samite, mystic,
    wonderful,
And caught him by the hilt, and
    brandish'd him.
Three times, and drew him under in
    the mere.'

Not the great thunder of a Niagara or a Victoria, but a thin-lipped fury, a mare's tail lashing between rocks. Each of these falls has inspired a pen — George Borrow wrote of Pistyll Rhaeadr (*below*) in Clywd that he had never seen 'water falling so gracefully, so much like thin beautiful threads as here', and it is indeed the most magnificent waterfall in Wales.

Wordsworth was much enamoured of Aira Force (*right*), near Ullswater, and set *The Somnambulist* here. The ribbon of rainbow falling across the fierce white waters certainly creates that kind of mystical effect of which he was so fond, as indeed does the exquisite misty stillness of Great Langdale Beck (*centre below*).

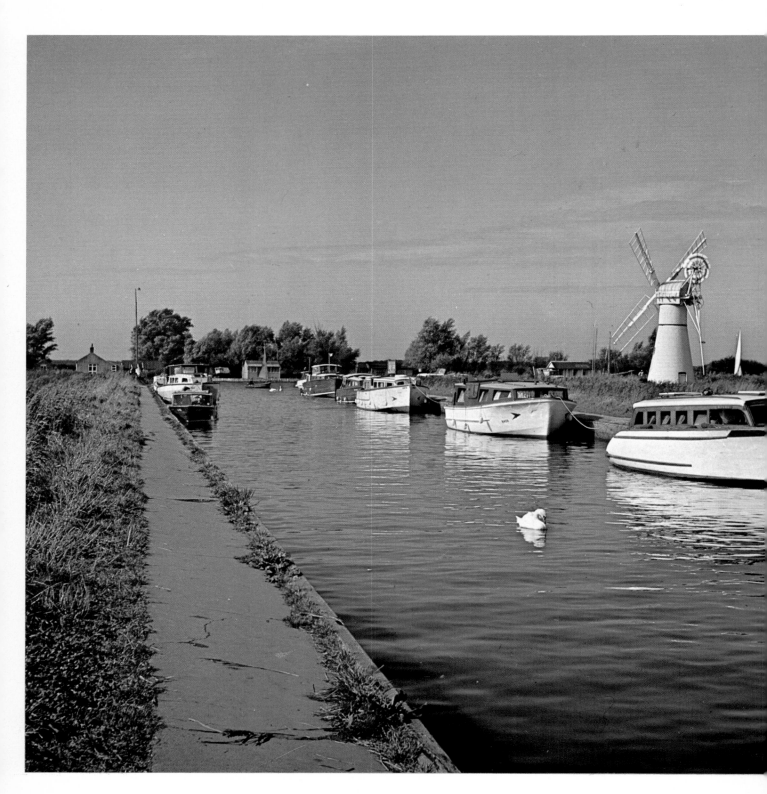

Man has made roads and runways and in the process more often than not has massacred the landscape, but where he has made rivers he has usually enhanced it. The dyke by Thurne Mill on the Norfolk Broads (*below left*) may have an austere straightness to it, and the heavy machinery at Laggan Locks (*below*) in Inverness-shire may seem a little cumbersome, but both lend favour to the eye when it sweeps the terrain looking for that strip of silver water, be it lake, river, canal, waterfall or duckpond, which so attracts the British for some deep-down reason, some subterfuge emotion buried far back in the race memory.

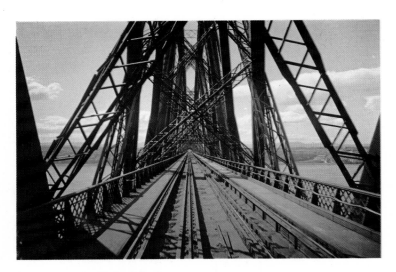

Away across the Firth of Forth
beneath the girders of its famous
railway bridge . . .

Acknowledgments

Peter Baker   49, 61, 111, 115

Barnabys Picture Library   39, 64 top, 72 top left, 90 top left

John Bethell   102/103

Roy Birks   124/125

G. Douglas Bolton   12, 20 top, 18, 58 top, 63 top, 66/67, 92/93, 108, 117, 118, 126

Vincent Brown   13 top, 31 top

Camera Press   86, 97

J. Allan Cash   16 bottom, 70 top, 75

Peter Cheze-Brown   17, 120/121, 122 left

Colour Library International   front cover top left and top right, 30, 31 bottom, 38/39

W. F. Davidson   contents page, 12/13 top, 14, 20 bottom, 19, 42, 44 top and bottom, 45, 47, 48 top, 50, 51, 52, 53, 54, 55, 56 (inset), 56/57, 59, 62, 63 bottom, 72/73 bottom, 74, 76, 78, 84/85, 87, 92 left, 93 right, 95 top, 96, 100 top and bottom, 101, 104/5, 107 top and bottom, 109, 110, 112, 119, 120 (inset), 122 right, 123 right, 125 right

Eagle Photos   13

V. K. Guy   82/83, 91

The Hamlyn Group Picture Library   title verso, 16 top, 24/25, 27 top and bottom, 33, 68/69, 71, 77, 80 top and bottom, 94, back cover top left

Jarrold and Sons Ltd   back cover top right and bottom

A. F. Kersting   28, 29, 58 bottom, 70 bottom, 81, 116

Keystone Press Agency   25 top left and right

David R. MacAlpine   48 bottom

Monitor Press Features Ltd   65, 95 bottom, 99

Picture Index   10, 88/89, 89 (inset)

Picturepoint Ltd   front cover bottom, half title page, 22/23, 26, 32, 34, 36/37, 60, 64 bottom, 103

Pix Photos   title page, 113 bottom

Kenneth Scowen   90 bottom, 98, 114

Skyport fotos   79, 113 top

John Woolverton   8/9, 11, 15, 21, 40/41, 46, 72/73 top, 73

ZEFA (U.K.) – E. G. Carle   35